MW01236180

Amanda

May these poems
bring you inspiration
in every day life
and while raising
your children.

Catherine Whitelock

Roses for Mother

Poems written by Alice Wallenfelsz Cline
A Depression Era Mother Living in Rural America
Compiled by Catherine Whelchel

Strategic Book Group

Copyright © 2011
All rights reserved – Catherine Whelchel

No part of this book may be reproduced or transmitted in any form or by any means, graphic, electronic, or mechanical, including photo-copying, recording, taping, or by any information storage retrieval system, without the permission, in writing, from the publisher.

Strategic Book Group
P.O. Box 333
Durham CT 06422
www.StrategicBookClub.com

ISBN 978-1-60976-977-2

Interior Page Design: Linda W. Rigsbee

Dedication

This book is dedicated to the children of
Alice Elizabeth Wallenfelsz and David Thomas Cline:
Cecil Robert Cline
Luada Elaine Cline Wesel
Grace Lois Cline Oppe
Dean David and Neil David Cline
(both deceased @ birth or shortly after).

And to the many rural American families who were able to
eke out a living during the Great Depression.

Table of Contents

Roses for Mother

Poetry by Alice Elizabeth Wallenfelsz Cline
A Depression Era mother living in rural America
Compiled by Catherine Whelchel

Preface

Alice Elizabeth Wallenfelsz Cline, born April 30, 1904, died December 25, 1953, attended Ohio University and graduated from Newspaper Institute of America, a school of journalism in New York City. She could read and write Spanish, German, and Italian as well as English. She loved nature and this comes across in her poetry. She was a grade school teacher at Little Muskingum Rural schools near Dart, Ohio. This was and still is a rural part of Ohio. She married David Thomas Cline and raised her family of three children on a farm in Wingett Run, Ohio. She was a Diamond level 4-H leader and Sunday school teacher in addition to work, farm, and family responsibilities. She died suddenly at the young age of forty-nine of a stroke on Christmas Day. The three living children reside in Ohio and West Virginia. Her son still lives on the land on which they were raised.

Her daughter, Luada Cline, like her siblings, was born and raised on the farm. She moved to Marietta after attending Ohio University. While working at the River Gas Company, she met and married Joseph Henry Wesel. They live in Marietta, Ohio and seven of their eight children are still living.

Luada's daughter, Catherine, discovered a box with papers from Alice Wallenfelsz Cline during preparation for a move and compiled this book of her poetry from them. This is believed to be a fairly complete compilation of the poetry of Alice Wallenfelsz Cline. Partial pieces of a few other poems were found but could not be pieced together. These include: "The Sky Road" and "The Village Widow." Catherine is a nurse living in South Carolina. She is married with three children of her own.

Acknowledgement

I would like to acknowledge my husband, Dick, for his patience and support throughout this "labor of love"—his name for the project. Especially, Dick, thank you for your assistance in naming and organizing the book in the eleventh hour. Also, much appreciation goes to my daughters: Catherine who helped with typing and Erica who helped with the tedious work of editing and proofing.

Finally, thank you, mom, for answering my countless questions and dad for encouraging me to publish.

Introduction

This book of poetry tells the story of the work and times on a rural farm in the 1930s and 40s during World War II. A number of the poems were printed in the *Marietta Times* and the *New Matamoras Enterprise* newspapers of that time.

Summer Breezes

Vacation Time

I love to watch the sunbeams
That dance about in play
Among your golden curls, dear,
When we two play croquet.
With mirth and play and laughter
We greet the Merry May
A toast—you are the winner
When we two play croquet.

Summer Is Here

The pleasant summer weather now
    is here
It brightens our lives with sunshine
    and cheer
The harvest hands seek cool shade
    for a rest
The Alder bush wears white hats
    on his crest
The guttler, that cold winter left so
    white
Are sporting green vines and
    dewberries bright
Sharp scythes and machines now
    swiftly lay
To earth the fragrant meadow crops
    of hay
From neighboring windows sly
    rabbits pass
Each seeking shelter in the standing
    grass
This is the theme the blue bird sings
    so clear
Sweet summer's here—Now is
    Sweet summer here.

A Watermelon

A verdant green among the leaves and grass
So softly now I pass
For fear that I should trample to the earth
The vine I judge its worth
Considering the drought, its immense size,
With glowing heart, I prize
It's wondrous beauty now surprising me
I test it just to see
If it could possibly be ripe;
It's fine. I clip it from the vine,
From an enfranchisement that lasted through.
The spring and summer too
I hold it in my arms and view the sky
That pilot with tri-motored plane and I
With equability keep tryst with God
He flies—I grow a melon from the sod.

Uncle Sam's Daughter

Written about the 4-H club, which Alice served as a 4-H club leader.
The club was named the Home Defense 4-H club for one year.
The name changed annually.

The little Club girls with baskets
Are hunting hillside o'er
To find and can the ripe berries
And fill, a few jars more.

The little girls are canning food
And helping "Uncle Sam"
To keep "Old Glory" . . . floating high
And make our enemies scram.

The little hands are searching yet
No fruits must wasted be,
Our soldier boys we'll surely feed
In camps, on land and sea.

The little "Home Defense" girls' plan
A victory to win,
Their home and country aiding much
When canning they begin.

The farmerettes! How they love to
Applaud the red, white, and blue!
Yea! Future wives of our farm boys
America's proud of you!

The Buckeye Girl

"Dedicated to little daughter, Grace Lois Cline, copyrighted 1945"
Published in the Ohio Poetry Anthology Publications
and the Marietta Times

Just to be a girl again
In the grand old "Buckeye" state;
Just to drive home the cows
Through the big, wide farmyard gate.

Just to row a'near the shore
In our ruby red canoe;
Just ramble o'er the hills
Of Ohio, dear, with you.

Just to view Ohio's banks
And to see the barges float;
Just to watch the white caps form
And ride in the ferry boat.

Just to hear the grinding noise
When the B&O goes by;
Just to sit on Dad's front porch
While the airplanes hum on high.

Just to stroll along the lane
There beneath the harvest moon;
When the katydids all sing
And all of the world's in tune.

Just to go hiking through the woods
Picnicking with you, my dears;
Where the oaks and sycamores
Whisper of brave pioneers.

Just to climb high Indian rocks
And hunt for flint arrow heads;
Gather lovely blossoms, too,
From their green moss-covered beds.

Just to be Ohio's girl
Swinging in the grapevine swing;
Just a girl whose heart is true
And free as the birds that sing.

The Gold Star Mother

Written for Alice's husband's maternal grandmother, Grandmother Newell.

Eyes that have grown dim with weeping
As on earth she toiled each day
Asking God to bless her dear boy
While each morning she knelt to pray.

But now she rests in that mansion
Which God has built in the skies
Watches and waits for His coming
For the soul we know never dies.

I know that somewhere in heaven
Just within the pearly gate
Is a place where all His angels
And the Gold Star mother's wait.

Lines to a Bee

Our Lord can never send to me
A lovelier insect than the bee.
She pollinates my pretty flowers
And working thru the daytime hours
Stores honey in the comb for me,
To sweeten cakes when I serve tea.
And from the comb comes wax you see
To help the farmer graft his tree.
She searches o'er the grassy lea,
For single blooms that we can't see.
The forest tree yields golden lore
That she has sorted for God's own poor,
She never gossips of a friend
But bravely works unto the end.
Oh, that our lives might daily be
As good and useful as the bee!

Fifth War Loan

Alice received a certificate in 1944 for her services as a volunteer in the sale of war bonds during the "Fifth War Loan Drive," which was held from June 12 through July 8, 1944. The certificate of recognition was from the war finance committee for Ohio and the United States Treasury Department.

I work for the Yanks in fighting ranks
And wounded warriors here
I am helping Uncle Sam each day,
For I'm a bondadier
I'm selling bonds to you and you
This war loan is coming fine
You do your bit and I'm glad of it,
So good soldier, I'll do mine.

My Gift of Nature

O Nature, with your balmy breeze
Your light ethereal air.
O nymphs of forest glade and trees
I find you everywhere.

O speak, yea speak, speak unto my soul
That I may dream of love
Of heaven, of God, of angels fair
Redeeming thrones above.

O pines with snow fairies white
That glisten in the air
Hold fast my soul in vision bright
Where every mortal's fair.

O heart that pines for happiness
O nature singing sleepily
Clasp tight again in fond embrace
The very soul of me.

Heritage of the Hills, a sonnet

A heritage of hills, green woods, is mine;
Of natures love divine;
So blessed by God's own hand and love
Abundant in their growth. Above
The clouds refreshen earth with falling rains.
The hills are rich with grains.
Flock after flock feeding in the pastures green
Where fragrant grass is seen;
Row after row of waving grains adorn
The fields. A world is born
Rich in the products of earth; blessed by God,
In Christ the solid rock. We mingle with the sod
When life is done. A tryst without a loss
Our bridges burned, we grasp, we hold, the cross.

Wings of Heaven (a song)

When the sun is sinking low
Day is ending here below
Wings of Heaven are watching over me.

Evening shadows drawing near
Songs of angels I can hear
Wings of Heaven are watching over me.

chorus:
Over me, over me
Wings of Heaven are watching over me
Watching, watching, watching over me
Wings of Heaven are watching over me.

When I draw the shutters near
Fluttering wings I always hear
Wings of Heaven are watching over me.

Shadows closer fall my way
Drawing closer every day
Wings of Heaven are watching over me.

chorus:
Over me, over me
Wings of Heaven are watching over me
Watching, watching, watching over me
Wings of Heaven are watching over me.

My faith upholds me everywhere
My songs float out on wings of prayer
Wings of Heaven are watching over me.

With my friend I'm not alone
When my Savior calls me home
Wings of Heaven will keep watch over me.

chorus:
Over me, over me
Wings of Heaven are watching over me
Watching, watching, watching over me
Wings of Heaven are watching over me.

Polly's Playhouse

Written for Alice's niece, Polly Cline Becker

Once upon a time
My niece Polly Cline
Thought she'd build a playhouse—
    Just for fun
Underneath the store,
With a little door
And arranged her toys—one by one.

Letters would arrive
From her playmates five,
In the wee mailboxes built with
    Care
All the summer long
With a merry song
They would spend their happiest hours there.

School began today,
Now no time for play
So they bid you little house
    "adieu."
When the winter's o'er
Roses round the door
They will build you, once again anew.

Good-By to the Drouth

Written after a terrible drought in the mid 1930s
(Drouth is the "old" word for drought)

Suddenly the drouth was broken
    Showers falling to the ground
      Suddenly the earth was softened,
Thirsty trees a drink had found.

Clear cool pools where birds may splatter,
    Puddles left for waddling ducks
      Water now for thirsty cattle,
Hang-ups washed for loaded trucks.

Good-by to the drouth forever
    Gladly now we see you go;
      God has sent the wonderful rain;
Come rain—shine sun—crops can grow.

If I Were a Fish

I'd like to be the little fish
    That nibbles at your hook,
For I would tease you Lydia as
    You fish within the brook.

I'd flash around in the sunlight there
    Almost within your reach;
And then when you would catch me
    I'd scamper for the beach.

I'd like to be a little fish
    Just for a day you see.
But 'spos'in I'd get caught why then
    A fish I wouldn't be.

I know you will forgive me, now
    For teasing you today;
But I must have my fun Lydia
    God made me just that way.

This foolish little poem here
    A lesson might evoke.
That he who first begins the fun
    Is worse hurt by the joke.

Little Chico

The following quote was found in Alice's papers: "Little Chico was a co-teacher in music and her rhythmical movements were so grand, I often thought of her as a Spanish boy in 4-H club camp and at school." In 4-H camp, "We went on bird walks before the breakfast bugle call."—Alice Cline.

All the newest songs you bring
And we love to hear you sing
For you make the music ring
                    Little Chico

We have climbed the steepest hill
And I say, don't you know I love you still
And I know, don't you know I always will
                    Little Chico

See the campfire on the hill
Yet the cold wind blows there still
While our songs the night air fill
                    Little Chico

Brilliant birds high in the trees
Smell of clover in the breeze
Bittersweet among the leaves
                    Little Chico

You may dress in silk and lace
Counting slacks not out of place
When our woodland paths we trace
                    Little Chico

We can hear the bugles cry
Watch "old glory" raised on high
With 4-H banner in the sky
                    Little Chico

My Mystical Dream

"These lines from 'My Mystical Dream' are written in kind loving memory of my dearest uncle, D. F. Wallenfelsz, who passed away November 23, 1943." —Alice Cline
Alice lived with her uncle, a physician, for a short time. A flu outbreak sent her home as many died from the flu at that time.

The last kiss is mine; the last kiss is mine;
The angels spoke softly to old Father Time.
Why was it thus when the death angel came
I could not see your face or hear your dear name?
I would empty the chalice of heartache and pain
I would kiss your pale lips till they answer again.
Was it only your spirit I kissed Uncle Mine?
When I lived in my dreams with the angels sublime?
I kissed you long dead—you laughed and you spoke,
And clasped tight my hand in a good hearty shake.

Oh, Uncle, dear Uncle, in dreams you were there
And we were so happy without even a care.
Sometimes I still hear you as often of yore
When you were too tired to go calling once more,
Yet the summons would come, "Send the doctor, please,"
And always as usual you answered all these;
"I must go, I am needed, I just wanted a sip
Of good coffee, Laura. Please fill my cup."
With your hat and your satchel, you walked away,
While there seemed no ending to the long weary day.
Your work was e'er guided by Him up above
Who constantly fills our hearts with His love.

There in the waiting room many sick patients stayed
While seeking advice and good medical aid.
I would dust all the bottles, while a patient you'd see
Put the office in order and clean carefully,
And all the small bottles that were empty, quite,
I'd refill with pills pink, yellow, and white.
Till everything shone in the office and shelves
Like the fairies had cleaned to amuse themselves.

The telephone rings and I answer it, too,
It might be from Ava, Caldwell, or Fairview,
Or maybe someone whom my auntie knew
Calling to chat, ask us to parties, too.
Then oft Polish people came calling for you
So little of Polish or Latin I knew,
I couldn't comprehend, so all I could say
Was, "please call again soon, the doctor's away."
I was but fourteen. In our small rural school
Only English was taught; the one language I knew.
I decided and vowed to myself there and then,
That someday when grown, I'd surely speak ten.

June

June came out to meet me
  With roses in her hair,
Her feet shone with the dew,
  Gray clouds were in the air.

I linked my arm with hers
  And danced across the lawn,
For I was happy in,
  The radiant rosy dawn.

June you are like a bride
  Adorned in her best,
Clad in a bright green gown,
  So becomingly dressed.

I love your grassy meads
  And fields of clover bloom;
Accept all royal regrets
  Dear June, you pass too soon.

Summer Breezes

There are breezes in treetops,
    In the orchard, in the lane,
There are breezes on the hilltops
    Rippling through the golden grain.
How the breezes fan the treetops!
E'en the treetops trimmed with care
Oh, the breezes touch the dew drops
    And the dew drops kiss the air.
There are little breezes blowing,
    You can find them everywhere
God sent summer breezes knowing
    They would waft away all care.

Somewhere It's Evening

Sorghum Time of Long Ago

Slipper Slap, Needles Eye, and Blind Man's Bluff
are children's games of that era.

October skies are bright with blue
The round full moon shines all night through.
Sweep off the dust, wash clean the pan
Now it's time for the 'lasses man.

We go to work with earnest will
And grind the cane the tubs to fill,
The tired old horse winds round the sweep,
While juice in the tubs gets deep, deep, deep.

The pans of juice are boiling thick,
The 'lasses man is whittling quick,
And making paddles bright and new
For small Marie, Joe, Jean, and Sue.

Out on the lawn the young folks cry
For "Slipper Slap" or "Needles Eye,"
And "Blind Man's Bluff," too finds a place
In shining eyes and eager face.

The farmer with his neighbor clicks
On weather, crops and politics.
The clock has rung the midnight chimes
Ere they relinquish "Good old times."

The syrup's cooked, the jars they fill
For valley home and highest hill;
There's twenty gallons made for each
And some the hundred mark may reach.

The tired old team winds round the road
With farmer folks, a gay young load.
The clock has struck the hour of two
Ere farm and home come into view.

The 'lasses man he comes and goes—
God's on His throne and well He knows
Popcorn and taffy gladdens swains
Mid wintry blasts on farms and plains.

Bloomfield Valley

Alice's children went to school and family activities in Bloomfield.

Where lacy mists arise in air
With lilting song birds everywhere
Where golden daisies view the sky
And running rivers meet the eye
Where forest nymphs in gay dress dance
By beauty fleetest furs enchance
The brook low murmurs with the trees
The wayside flowers feed the bees
At Bloomfield Valley.

The forest holds a style review
The trees are dressed in every hue
The maples are blonde, oh so fair
'Tis oaks that dark green color wear
Draft the breath of Jack Frost's sting
He will their autumn colors bring
The artist brush could e'er portray
The autumn forest's fall array
At Bloomfield Valley.

The fodder shocks all stand in row
Like soldiers that await the foe
The katydids beneath the moon
While yellow pumpkins meet their doom
Sumac's display their berries red
For winter birds must all be fed
The little squirrels are storing food
Within their nests of hollow wood
At Bloomfield Valley.

Above the creek upon a knoll
The modern school the youth enroll
The busses like yellow butterflies
With tints of rainbows from the skies
Now wind around the little dale
With boys and girls from hill and vale
And in their rooms most all the while
The teachers wear a pleasant smile
At Bloomfield Valley.

The little white church stands nearby
To prove that God is ever nigh
Within the homes through countryside
Where peace and faith and love abide
There's grandeur mid the Rockies breeze
And where the Colorado weaves
But wonders I dare you to find
That's grander than I have in mind
At Bloomfield Valley.

And softly twilight shadows fall
On flowers, trees, and over all
They chase the changing streets of lights
Across the path of moonbeams bright
And when the angels whisper low
Say unto me, "'Tis time to go,"
My last long breath shall then depart
Ere that calm valley leaves my heart
At Bloomfield Valley.

Cute Paper Dolls

Three lovely wee first grade girls
Each learning A B C's
And wearing anklets pretty
And pinafores near knees

Each cutting paper dollies
All sorts of fol de rols
Each cutting toys to color
And pretty paper dolls

Now Wilma cuts a factory
With airships big to fly
And Norma cuts a city
With ancient castles high

Now Grace cuts out a schoolhouse
With rooms for every grade
She is superintendent
Recording progress made

Each one tip-toeing forward
Comes now to teacher's desk
"Please, may we have the scissors?"
Three busy students blessed.

My Valley Home

Alice wrote this poem about her home on Clinevale farm in Wingett Run, Ohio.

There's a little white house in the valley
That a wreathe of green meadows entwine
There's a little farmhouse in the valley
An' I call that little home mine.

'Tis there when the glorious sun set
Vanished at close of the day
That the household bade you "Welcome"
Eat, rest, and be glad and gay.

And far on the high hills surrounding
The tall pines beckon and sway
Like tall soldiers guarding the valley
And the little white house today.

In that little white house in the valley
When my work and chores are through
And I sit in the coolness of evening
Darling I'm thinking of you.

Wabash Blues

This poem was inspired after a car trip to Wisconsin to visit relatives when Alice crossed Wabash River.

It is moonlight on the Wabash
Happy journey all the way,
But my heart is in Ohio
And I'm going there today.

It is moonlight on the Wabash
Gay canoes beneath a tree,
But my heart is in Ohio
Someone's waiting there for me.

It is moonlight in Lake County
Bright lights shine high in the air
For the county fair's in progress
And the crowds have gathered there.

For Lake County's race track circles
All around a little lake
And the moonlight on the waters
Nature's grandest beauty make.

All around Lake County's race track
Ponies prancing to and fro
Boys and girls are gaily calling
"Giddyap" and "Whoa there, whoa."

It is moonlight on the Wabash
Hoosiers river ripples blue
But my heart is in Ohio
So I'm merely passing through.

It is moonlight on the Wabash
How the night winds fan the trees
And my inner conscience whispers
Ah! How beautiful are these!

It is moonlight on the Wabash
Aye, how perfect was the day;
But my heart is in Ohio
And I'm glad I'm on my way.

That's Why I Am a Tramp

*It was not uncommon for tramps to come to the farm homes
and ask for a slice of bread with jelly. The following poem
was inspired by these visits.*

I have a simple story
Yet it is hard to tell,
Once joy with love and kindness
But now a gleam of hell.

I know what others call me,
A tramp I hear them say,
He's dirty old and ragged
I'll send him on his way.

Now listen to my story
There was a little lad
Who stolen from home and mother
By robbers bold and bad.

Was smuggled in a big ship
Upon the ocean bound,
And locked within a prison
Where he could not be found.

About three days they kept him
Without a bite to eat
Then all they gave the laddie
Was wine and brandy sweet.

'Twas there he learned the habit
To drink, to smoke, to chew
To play with cards and gamble
Yes stranger, it is true.

Forgotten home and mother
Forgotten comrades too,
And drinking, stealing, swearing
The only arts he knew.

At last the ship has landed
Upon a foreign shore
The cruel pirates left him
They were his friends no more.

There he was seized by others
And carried far within
A land that they call Darfur
A new life to begin.

He worked from morn till evening
And never got no pay
They tied him to the whipper
And whipped him every day.

One day the fates had given
The chance he longed for yet
He ran away from Darfur
As far as he could get.

The cruel slaves were chasing
He hoped he might be free.
The enemy was coming
His only hope the sea.

One moment hesitated
Then leaped into the sea
He longed for home and freedom
He longed for liberty.

A passing ship discovered
A tiny floating speck
They lower, now, the lifeboat
They haul him to the deck.

They were his friends and comrades
"The good old U.S.A."
I think that God had sent them
To help the run-away.

His hopes were fast returning
That he might once again
Behold his own dear mother
Behold his native land,

But there was war then, stranger
On land and on the sea,
And ere he reached America
They met the enemy.

Haul down the stars and stripes
They called within a pace
But when the ship was sinking
Old Glory held her place.

He watched her slowly sink, then
His hope of liberty
That flag still gave him courage
To brave the stormy sea.

Not long until they found him
And landed him at home
A country he was proud of
That he might call his own.

A raging fever seized him
Until he nearly died
No mother there to comfort
Or hear him when he cried.

But now that he is better
He is searching far and wide
Yes, for his angel mother
And he,—is at your side.

Yes I'm that boy, that stranger
That's why I'm a tramp
That's why I walk from day to day
That's why I'm cold and damp.

If I may sit by your fire
A bite of dinner get
And dry my clothes and feet sir
For they are soaking wet.

I thank you many times, sir
I never shall forget
And I'll be on my way, and
I may find my mother yet.

To a Tortoise

Brave little tortoise walking
    slow
You never hurry when you go.
Substantial home, you carry too
From enemies, you're hid from
    view.

Though you are slow you win the
    race
By measured step and steady pace.
A lesson you should teach to all
As o'er the earth you daily
    crawl.

Threshing Time

With a chug, chug, chug, the tractor
   hums,
 To a dozen tasks the farmer runs,
And into the sacks, the black grain comes,
   When buckwheat's ripe in the valley.

With a heigh, heigh, ho, the miller
   hums,
And out through the sieve the fine flour comes,
And into the cake the batter runs,
   When buckwheat's ripe in the valley.

To the table now the platter comes
 And over the cakes, the syrup
   runs,
And oh! How we fill our tummy tums
   When buckwheat's ripe in the valley.

The Lost Schoolhouse

They tore the old school down dear,
    And hauled it all away
Now green wheat field is growing
Where once we used to play.

They built a modern brick one
    In town to take its place
The old one was falling down
They wanted no disgrace.

Our thoughts must not turn backward
    Must think ahead today
All our golden memories
They ought not take away

They tore the old school down dear,
    'Tis not remains to see
The modern brick is grand but—
The difference to me.

Love

Written while Alice was teaching fifty-four second graders.

Do you know the little school girl
That her playmate gave a shove
Know her little heart is lonely
For a little bit of love?

Do you know the wounded soldier
Gazing at the stars above
Prays to God from out the foxhole
For a little bit of love?

Do you know the weary farmer
As he works with God above
Feeds his flocks, yet too is lonely
For a little bit of love?

Do you know the school ma'am
With her smiles sent from above
As she guides her pupils, wishes,
Wishes for a little bit of love?

Do you know the little kitten
Too, is watched by Him above
When he drinks his milk is thankful
For a little bit of love?

Do you know the weary patient
From his cot looks up above
Longs for home and human kindness
And a little bit of love?

Do you know the wide world's daily
Praying for the throne above
Do you know the whole world's dying
For a little bit of love?

Armistice Day

Ah, how well do I remember
How the church bells all were rung;
On a day one sad November
And the message that they brung.

Ah, they rang so loud and clearly;
Peace, peace, they seemed to say
And Americans love dearly
Precious news, they brought that day.

How America was cheering;
Knowing that the strife would cease.
"Over there" think how endearing,
"Peace" the blessed news of peace.

Halloween

*Written about Luada after Cecil and his friend dressed in scary clothes
one Halloween and frightened her.*

A little girl lay sleeping
Upon her little bed;
The little girl was dreaming
And this, is what she said,

"Away old ghosts and goblins
With black cats chasing you;
Go away old pumpkin faces,
And wicked witches too."

She kicks the bedpost soundly,
And throws her pillow too;
Then pounds her fists together
And slumbers all night through.

The father kissed his child, then
Her antics he had seen;
Said to the worried mother
Too much of Halloween.

A Song of Youth

O sing me a song of the mountains
O sing me a song of the hills
O sing me a song of girlhood dreams
Of rapture, of joy, and thrills.

O sing, of the birds in the treetops
O sing, of the squirrels at play
O sing, of the green grass and meadows
And later the new mown hay.

O sing, of the bees in the clover
O sing, of the brooks in bloom
O sing, of the brooks that babbling
And crowding the banks for room.

O sing, me a song, half a mile long
Aye, sing of young dreams that I own
O sing of the peace and quietude
O sing of a country home.

A November Hurricane

Without a warning, winter came
The soft snow filled the air
The harsh winds hurried down the vale
Yet blowing everywhere.

The cattle hurried home because
'Twas stormy overhead
The sheep and lambs sought shelter as
They scurried to the shed.

A blanket of the purest white
O'er all the earth was spread
The brooks had ceased their murmuring
The stars had gone to bed.

The faithful heart is unafraid
Above the lashing storm
The voice of God speaks to us all
His wonder to perform.

The Soul Light

Little white light, that shines very bright
That light in your soul and mine;
That gift from above, of heaven's love,
That leads to the Christ divine.

This light all aglow, shows where to go
Though the road be dark or drear;
Never go wrong, fill your life with song,
And Christ will be always near.

Lamps aflame, enlightening Christ's name
To the world the Gideon's gift;
Follow that gleam, that bright beacon's beam,
That to heaven our souls lift.

To sheep gone astray this light each day
Welcomes to the great white throne;
Hold fast to the light like stars at night,
With Christ you'll not walk alone.

Like the gold lamp looks, on Gideon books
That gives you God's precious truth;
This white light guides to a paradise,
Oh accept it now in youth.

In that precious Gideon book, I love to look
And I thank you day by day
For this comforting cheer, words so dear,
Teaching God's Christ-loving way.

Where the Silver-leafed Maples Grow

Nestled among the hills of Ohio
Is a quaint log cabin that I know
And I love that spot,
    And the queer small lot
Where the silver-leafed maples grow.

Each leaf glistens brightly like sunshine.
Each sways as the cooling breezes blow.
In my dreams I see,
    And I long to be
Where the silver-leafed maples grow.

When the summer days are—oh, so hot.
When the corn blades shrivel in the row
I'd toss you my hoe,
    'Tis there I would go
Where the silver-leafed maples grow.

In that quaint log cabin in the hills
Dwells a dear old auntie that I know,
And I love that place,
    And the kindly face
Where the silver-leafed maples grow.

What Do We Study For?

By Luada Elaine Cline
Written for Ohio Poetry Day by Alice's daughter, in eighth grade.

The other day I chanced to hear,
Two girls arguing oe'r and oe'r
One girl said to the other girl,
"What do you say we study for?"

"The highest grades in class,"
She said, "our education, dear,
When grace and manners accompany,
Desires to be helpful down here."

On God's industrial, earthly globe,
Dear student, there's work for the best,
If we are willing, upright and true,
Then our work will arouse the rest.

Our schooldays soon will be over,
And graduation's drawing near;
A chain of golden memories,
For us to hold forever dear.

Good citizens, our country needs,
In time of war and dire distress
Good students make good citizens,
That's what we study for, I guess.

Somewhere It's Evening

Somewhere the leaves are turning
Somewhere the tall pines sway
Somewhere a clean wind's blowing
Somewhere, somewhere, today.

Somewhere the day is ending
Somewhere the table's spread
Somewhere the lowly farmer
Gives thanks for daily bread.

Somewhere a God is watching
A God who loves us all
Somewhere His hand is guiding
He will not let us fall.

Alice Wallenfelsz Cline with husband David, daughters Grace and Luada

Luada Cline

The Cline family: Cecil, Alice, David, Grace, and Luada

Alice Elizabeth Wallenfelsz Cline, poetry author

Luada, Cecil and Grace, taken in Marietta in 2010.

Alice Wallenfelsz Cline in her wedding portrait.

Luada, Grace and Cecil Cline, taken in the yard of their home, Clinevale farm.

Peace

A New Year's Prayer

Written during World War II

A new year's dawning
May it bring peace
And warring nations
Their fighting cease.

We ask His guidance
We plead and pray
That to all nations
He'll show the way;

For war and fighting
And feuds to cease
And all the world will
Remain in peace.

February

February's come again
Bringing birthdays of great men
Washington and Lincoln too
Were once small boys just like you.

Longfellow, the poet great
His birth too, we celebrate
As you sit in school today
Do not fool your time away.

Lindberg found when he dared to fly
There is a way if you but try.
Don't trust luck as some folks say
Luck is out of style today.

Fame won't come, boys, over night
Those who work with brain and might
Will find while they climb up hill
There's a way if there's a will.

February we're glad you're here
Shortest month of the year
Though your days be cold and drear
We read books while you are here.

Youth

Written for Cecil, Alice's son; his horse was named Ben.

A holiday; no school for him
Delightful day! So full of vim
With bow and arrow he hunts game
A youth at large a youth the same.

Who drives the cows along the lane
And rides old Ben with flowing mane
He helps with chores and studies too
And paints a picture for small Sue.

Then 'neath the nut tree with his sack
And carries home upon his back
Enough to last the winter through
And share with other small friends, too.

He hates to wash his freckled face
Or tie a stringy long shoe lace
He'd rather hunt some frogs or fish
Than help his sister wipe a dish.

Two small brown hands that help his dad
A farmer's boy, a romping lad
With light brown eyes and rumpled hair
A happy boy, he knows no care.

Chore Time

There was a dinner bell, which was used on the farm
to call in working family from the field. 'Spotty' was the name
given to a cow on their farm.

The robin sings so rhythmic
Mid lilacs on the lawn;
The farmer and his horses
Have plowed a field since dawn.

The supper bell is ringing
The harness jingles now—
And hay the farm boys pitching
From lofts above the mow.

The horses haste to water
They've earned a rest and feed;
The cows are coming homeward
With Spotty in the lead.

Out there beyond the meadow
The lambs still frisk and play;
And hovered close together
The little chickens stay.

With dainty eats and dishes
The table there is spread,
And with his happy family
The farmer breaks the bread.

Baby Slippers

Written about her daughter, Grace.

Little tripper here's your slippers
I have mended them; you see
Every stitch was neatly taken
So that you might happy be.

Little tripper, with your slippers
Skipping here and there, in play
May your life be bright and sunny
And your paths be always gay.

Little tripper, with your slippers
Golden curls and bright blue eyes
Rosy cheeks and baby dimples
You're the treasure that we prize.

Ohio! Ohio! Ohio! (A song)

*The 49th state, Alaska, was not added to the United States
as a state until 1959. (Copyright 1946)*

Ohio! Ohio! Ohio!
Happy homes and lovely trees
Rivers rambling round the hills
Where old glory greets the breeze.

Chorus:
Ohio! Ohio! Ohio!
Let us cheer our lovely state
Heigh-ho! Heigh-ho! Ohio!
With her many heroes great.

Ohio! Ohio! Ohio!
Let her hills and valleys ring
Celebrate our country's birth
Let her sons and daughters sing.

Ohio! Ohio! Ohio!
Reapers cleaning golden sheave
Buckeye trees and giant oaks
Stand arrayed in shining leaves.

Ohio! Ohio! Ohio!
Bringing memories so grand
Dearest state of forty-eight
God keep freedom in her land.

My Calendar for 1938

Gay calendar with numbers bright
Ah! Could I only see
The joy and grief that you may bring,
Woulds't gaze so frequently?

But as I hold you in my hands
And leaf your pages through,
I only pray for strength to bear
The tasks He bids me do.

Ay, strength to help a stumbling soul,
Along the narrow way,
That as I lift another's load,
I lift my own today.

Yea, banish all the trifling cares
That are not worth a fret,
May this year find me nobler grown
Than any year as yet.

I would not want too much of joy
There must be clouds—a few
To darken sunny paths awhile,
God knows and sends them too.

And as I gaze upon the days
'Tis comforting to know;
My Father's Hand is leading me
Wherever I may go.

The Dreaming Catalpas

I know you dear Catalpa trees
You're tired of winter's rough, cold breeze,
With your rain-washed gray leafless boughs,
You're dreaming dreams that will arouse
The tiny buds from winter's sleep,
Now whispering softly "peep, peep, peep."
You dream of spring and birds and bees
Oh, don't you now, you dear old trees!

Five friendly trees with lovely ways
Where robin sings, his family sways
Each summer day, you shade the street
For graying heads and little feet
On quiet eves, when day is done
The village rests from noise and hum.
Far overhead the night hawk sails
With mournful voice he wails and wails.

And when the cold winds wintry blow
Dream not, in sunny climes you grow
But be content just where you stand
God wants you here, 'twas His command;
That you should grace the village street
To gladden hearts of children sweet,
For that dear Lord who cares for me
He lives again within a tree.

Oh, dream of sunlight's faltering rays
Through brilliant phantom flower sprays
Inspiring love for forest glade
To all who rest beneath your shade
Look up, dear trees, to stars above
Dream now of war, our life and love
Dream on, dear trees, still whispering
"Wee buds unfold; I hail thee spring."

Violinist's Promise

Oh, the times that you have promised
Just to come and play for me
Some gay ballad of the northland
Or an Irish melody.

And sometimes when it is evening
And I sit and rest at ease,
I can hear those Golden Slippers
Floating on the evening breeze.

And at times when I am dreaming
In some far off pleasant land,
I can hear the gentle drumming
Of the notes by your fair hand.

Oh the times that you have promised
Just to come and play for me,
But each promise you have broken
For your face I never see.

Christmases

This poem was written when Luada was in sixth grade, around 1942.
She was asked to memorize a poem for a Christmas play
and her mother wrote this poem for her.

Could I but visit Washington
   On Christmas Eve at dark,
And glimpse the public Christmas tree
   That stands within the park.

Could I but see the White House tree
   Within the East room there,
With its electric lights all lit
   And bright star hung with care.

I'd think of other Christmases
   That now are past and gone,
And view the lovely portraits
   That the bright light falls upon.

I'd think of Alice Tyler then
   Who "good and bad and worst",
With other little children there
   Her Christmas play would rehearse.

Of dearest Dolly Madison
   Who hung the mistletoe,
Where Mistress Adams—Abigail—
   Hung washing—long ago.

And then of young Tad Lincoln, who
   A hunger march did lead,
Procured for all his followers
   A regular Christmas feed.

See red-haired Tom Jefferson
   With fiddle and his bow,
Here that gold piano now sets
   You don't dare to touch, you know.

And see the Christmas carolers
   In red and green all dressed,
Who serenading White House folks
   Are caroling their best.

Alas! I cannot visit there
   For I have pies to bake,
A dinner, too, to plan and cook
   A Christmas gift to make.

Still I can trim our little pine
   Within our humble home,
And watch the Christmas star—that star
   For centuries has shone.

And I can feel the rapture of
   Small arms about my neck,
And hear the exclamation
   Look! Santa's come, by heck!

In Marietta

Marietta is located in the southeastern corner of Ohio and was the closest town of any size to Wingett Run, where the Clines lived. The Campus Martius Museum in Marietta has preserved the Rufus Putnam house. Visitors may tour it when visiting the museum.

There, when the western sunset glows
The stars arise and soft wind blows,
The whispering trees their stories tell
Of pioneers we loved so well.
Each waving leaf a scene portrays
Near Colonel Washington's surveys
Each tells a tale for me alone
Of Indian belief unknown
                              In Marietta.

And Putnam cabin in the shade
Where romping youngsters laughed and played,
In speaking, to that grandest elm,
No other tree can overwhelm,
Is spreading well the wondrous tale
And whispering softly of each vale
Near where, Ohio's silver crest
Engulfs the "Hudson of the West,"
                              In Marietta.

Oh whis'pring trees! Repeat your tale,
And sing it gladly down the vale.
Oh sing! Of heroes—gone before—
Of Washington,—and hundreds more.
Speak softly—of another time,
When sleeping soldiers stood in line,
And fought for home, and freedom too
Yet won this glorious land for you
                    In Marietta.

Yea! Gay old oaks, yea, speak again
Of all these heroes who were men;
Of covered wagons going west
To settle land that we love best;
Of Clark, of Putnam, others too,
Who made this land a home for you,
O Putnam cabin! Whisper well,
To all these trees your story tell
                    In Marietta.

O sycamores! Forget him not,
The farmer who would guard his lot,
With gun upon his shoulder pressed
He fought for all he loved best.
A whisper floats upon the breeze,
And says, so sweetly, all of these
Recorded here will live again
In history, hearts and minds of men
                    In Marietta.

Mother's Gift

I want to send my mother dear
A little gift today;
All made of gay bright calico
To wear on Mother's Day.
And way up in the corner here,
I'll pin a little note,
"Love to my own good mother dear,"
The message that I wrote.

I Plant a Tree

Written after Alice planted a tree in the yard.

Aye Arbor Day! A task for me;
How beautiful to plant a tree!
A tree whose lips can sip with ease
Sweet nectar that the clouds release,

Whose leaves will dance beneath the moon
To tunes the whippoorwills shall croon;
Whose leafy boughs shall house in spring
A home where robin reigns supreme.

Oh, I shall plant a dozen trees
A ship to sail upon the seas.
Aye, I shall plant a small canoe
And paddles, dipping in the blue.

I'll plant a little house that's new
A table and a chair or two,
And near my home a pretty pine,
To grace my yard in winter time.

A tree when winter's wind doth blow
Shall wear a dress of purest snow.
A task with joy unbound for me;
How beautiful to plant a tree!

December

December is a goddess
Upon a great white throne
The frozen brooks are jewels
That she claims for her own.

Her winds mid trees so barren
Make music everywhere
Unsung her grandest lyrics
Are broadcast on the air.

The snowy hills and mountains
Are pearls all set with care
The soft gray clouds are bonnets
That shield her silken hair.

She trips in very softly
You scarcely know she's here
She passes out as quickly
And crowns the glad New Year.

In Remembrance

There is a road, a narrow road
    That leads us unto God
That road is straight, that road is long,
That earthly saint must trod.

The narrow road leads heavenward
    Where with undying Love,
The Babe of Bethlehem awaits
To welcome us above.

That Babe who loved each race and creed,
    With His unselfish Love,
Doth still supply each earthly need
Still beckons us above.

And on His Birthday let's give thanks
To Him who gives us grace;
    And pray when this life here is done
We'll see His Blessed face.

My Castle of Dreams

In building castles in dreamland
Four angels keep guard at the gate
My castle gates swing outward
Each evening at half after eight.

Steps to my castle in dreamland
Were built by great masters of art
And you may enter my threshold
If you have true love in your heart.

Keys to my castle in dreamland
Are clasped tight in a little hand
And winsome baby smiles greet you
As wider my dream gates expand.

Then when the sand man comes stealing
And scatters his sand far and near
And angels whisper, "Sweet dreams,"
So gently to the children dear.

Deep in my castle dreamland
In deepest depths of my heart
I'll keep you forever and aye
And never shall let you depart.

Johnny's Letter

A mother trimmed her Christmas tree
With gifts and toys for children three.
Beneath the tree she saw a note
And this is what young Johnny wrote,
"I'm lonesome Santa as can be
Oh please bring Daddy home to me."
The snow had spread a carpet white
Footsteps led to their door that night.
The knob slow turns, a soldier brave
One foot left in a foreign grave,
Stands crippled yet he's bringing cheer
For he is home with loved ones dear.

Peace

Her only son; He joined the strife
Endangering his dear young life
Returneth not; she doesn't see,
The stirring breeze, or old oak tree,
The love of him who sits near by
And wipes a tear drop from his eye,
Great agony is in her breast.
She visits France and there finds rest.
She seeks a grave on foreign sod
Clings to the cross and prays to God
Her soul at last has found release
Lips form the words, "I am at peace."

Untold Joy

Roses for Mother

Surely I must visit the florist
And place my order this way:
"Twelve American beauty roses
For the dearest of mothers today."
Each petal will tell her I love her
Though her hair is silver gray;
Each leaf will say "God bless her"
Love and keep her safe always.

As each stem gives life to the rosebud,
She gave of her love to me;
Each thorn helps remind her of sorrow
I caused, when a child at her knee.
So I will care for and cherish,
Mother, loveliest of all today
Greatest of blessings is Mother
Who first taught our lips to pray.

The Flood

Written about the terrible flood of the Ohio River in 1937

Ohio's lovely valleys
Were ruffed by winter's breeze
And slowly streams were flowing
On toward distant seas.

The towns lay calm and peaceful
Along the river's way
The people well and happy
Were working day by day.

The clouds soon hid the sunshine
The rain kept falling down
Till earth was drenched with water
For many miles around.

The streamlets overflowing
Kept rushing to the sea
Till all the swollen rivers
Were loaded heavily.

Each river over-burdened
New banks began to find
Thus bringing great destruction
And sorrow to mankind.

The homes were left in darkness
Amid the water's gloom;
And guards were aiding helpless
By boat and food and room.

The Red Cross women working
The little children fed
Providing food and shelter
For each wee homeless head.

The chemists at the college
Were working night and day
For in pure drinking water
The people's safety lay.

When slow receding waters
With mud and filth passed on
Oh there were thousands homeless
And many loved ones gone.

The world with aid is ready
Throughout the USA
To help the stricken homeless
In sympathy today.

We pray mid this destruction
That God will still prove kind
And homes that tasted sadness
Most happy lives may find.

For oft when left in sorrow
We see the truth and light
And often comes from darkness
New strength to do the right.

Time-Honored Marietta

Time-honored Marietta
Thy walls to us are dear,
Oh, how can we forget thee,
Or the time that we've spent here,
Thy name we'll ever cherish,
And for thy banner fight,
Nor ever let it perish—
The Navy Blue and White.

Chorus:
Thy dear name we'll ever cherish,
And for thy banner fight,
Nor ever let it perish—
The Navy Blue and White.

Gladly do we sing thy praises
And of thy heroes tell—
How many brave hearts struggled
Because they loved thee well.
'Twill be our firm endeavor
To stand up for the right,
Protect, and keep thee ever,
O Navy Blue and White.

Lines on Memorial Day

Memorial Day is here again
With speeches, parades, flags flying: But then
The one-armed soldier is dearest to my heart
I say—
Than speeches by great men on Memorial Day.

Memorial Day has come again:
With its crowds of women, children, and men;
But brokenhearted mothers are nearer to my heart
I say—
Than cheering crowds on Memorial Day.

Memorial Day; we hear music roll
Yet the soldier's sweetheart whose unmated soul,
Though alive—though dead is far dearer
I say—
Than stirring music on Memorial Day.

Memorial Day with speech and band;
And little white crosses that dot the land—
But what should be dearer to all hearts
I say—
Than stirring music on Memorial Day.

Memorial Day with speech and band;
And little white crosses that dot the land—
But what should be dearer to all hearts
I say—
Is the nation they fought for, on Memorial Day.

Class Poem (1948)

Written for the graduation of her daughter, Luada

So you want me to tell you
About the class of forty-eight,
We've finally reached the goal
We're proud to graduate.

I'm sure it is the best class
That's graduated yet.
And of course it is the best one
That ever will I bet.

First comes Mary Thomas
A sweet attractive lass
She has a smile for everyone
And is head of every class.

Now here comes Dean Hall
With such wavy red hair
He is very popular
With lots of dates to share.

Last comes Luada Cline
She's tall and quite shy
Always ready with a smile
For every passerby.

Next comes Elma Bowser
The shortest of our class
Yet in many fine arts
The rest of us she'll pass.

Here's lovely Jean Yonally
Up-to-date clothes and curly hair
Her voice thrills all the audience
When her songs float on the air.

Next comes Chester Thomas
Quite popular he seems
He has a smile for every girl
And haunts them in their dreams.

Now here is Charles Morris
A carpenter at heart
The lips of all the ladies
Sing the praises of his art.

Next comes James Armstrong
A tall good-natured lad
He's fond of teasing all the girls
So he is never sad.

We hate to say good-bye to all
But the parting has to come
We've had to study very hard
Yet we've had lots of fun.

We cannot grieve at parting
For we're coming back some day
And greet our under classmates
As alumni some other May.

Spring Gardens

The deep blue sky is bending
To touch the earth below
The sun great warmth is sending
To help my garden grow.

For oh, I have a garden
Where lovely young plants grow,
Where little paths run sweetly
Beside the long, straight row.

My garden's full of dreamin'
And bird songs never cease
My vision is a cellar
Where shining jars increase.

My garden must have flowers—
They beautify our souls—
God smiles upon my garden
His benediction rolls.

When agony he suffered
The soul of man to save
Our Savior chose a garden
For His dear, lonely grave.

They laid Him in that garden
In far Gethsemane.
In every dew-washed flower
His tear-stained face, I see.

The women love the gardens
They daily tend and hoe,
May God His many blessings
Upon them all bestow.

In Memory of Neil David Cline

(Alice's infant son) Luada told me that she remembered her mother
sitting up and writing this the night the infant died. It was part
of his obituary.

The golden gates were open
And heavenly angels smiled
And with their tuneful harp string
Welcomed the little child.

They shouted high and holy,
A child hath entered in,
And safe from all temptation,
A soul is sealed from sin.

They led him through the golden streets
On to the King of Kings
And a glory fell upon him,
From the rustling of their wings.

The Savior smiled upon him
As none on earth had smiled.
And the heaven's great glory shown around
The little earth-born child.

On earth they missed the little one,
They sighed and wept and sighed,
And wondered if another such
As theirs had ever died.

Oh! Had they seen through those high gates
The welcome to him given
They never would have wished their child
Back from his home in heaven.

My Playmate

Written about her daughter, Grace.

I have a shining table new
And two chairs I call mine
Out on the lawn each sunny day
My dollies and I dine.

Now Nyla Jean just loves to come
And stay with me for tea;
And Patty is my dearest doll
We chat quite busily.

Ruth Annie is my cutest doll
Though she is very small
She only came last Christmas, so
I love her best of all.

My kitty stretches on the grass
Her blue eyes at us stare
As much as if to say "Sweet Miss,
Have you any milk to spare?"

But "Skeeter" is my fondest pet
Each morn at half past four
He wakens all the farmer folk
By crowing o'er and o'er.

Let other youngsters go to school
Next birthday I'll be four
I've pets and dolls and picture books
What child could wish for more?

Queen of My Heart (a song)

Among my dreams
There reigns a queen,
The one queen of my heart,
And through my dreams
Of all the years,
You're mine till death doth part;
Because you're mine alone my love,
The one queen that I own.
In my strong arms
I'll carry you within our own home.
I sealed our vows with one sweet kiss,
The parson made you mine,
And through our years of wedded bliss,
Those memories will shine

And if red roses mix with gold
And those golden bells should ring,
In golden scenes we reap in dreams
Rewards the years should bring.

Red roses in our corsages are wondrous works of art.
I crowned you with a crown of love,
I pressed you to my heart . . .

And if red roses mix with gold
And those golden bells should ring,
In golden scenes we reap in dreams
Rewards the years should bring.

What Is June

There was the nicest little boy
    Whose Christian name was Dwight
He went to see a little girl,
    'Most every Sunday night.

She dwelt beyond the grassy mead,
    And down a little lane
She waited by the gate for him,
    Her name was Sally Jane.

There were so many pleasant times
    Among their childhood years
But like the lofty lanky bridge
    With its great wooden piers.

Old father time is surely swift
    He passes oh, so soon!
'Twas only May a while ago
    And now it's rosy June,

So youth and love Sally Jane
    Won't pace a while I ween,
The roses were in bloom again
    And she was sweet sixteen.

He slipped upon her finger
    I'll bet you could not guess
They drove away to town next day
    With dapple gray and Bess.

They were happy all the while
    And toiled all the day long

There were trials and troubles, but,
    Their hearts were filled with song.

They gave the world a blessing rare
    Those seven sons so brave
But one is sleeping overseas
    An unknown soldier's grave.

One is dwelling in the west,
    Another is in Rome.
Two live within the distant city
    The other two are home.

Yet death came fleeting by
    Like some swift fairy gnome
And carried their father away
    To some fair heavenly home.

And Sally Jane sits in her chair
    With knitting by her side
She knits to pass the time away
    Till she can cross the tide.

Her hair has bleached to snowy white.
    And she is old and lame
But she was good and kind to all
    We love her just the same.

And what is June folks will ask,
    And we can say, Ah! Well
Come over here along with me
    I'm sure Grandma can tell.

My Ohio

Beautiful stars where old glory flies
Majestic waters that match the blue skies
Brilliant flowers with autumn's haze
Scarlet carnations, sunniest days
       My Ohio

Happiest homes where children play
Beautiful cars upon the highway
Friendliest roads that go winding along
Harmonious birds so happy with song
       My Ohio

Blessed old hills and beautiful trees
Shining bright colors in autumn's breeze
Yellowest sunshine, down-pouring rain
Bringing harvests of golden grain
       My Ohio

Scattered snowflakes that fly through the air
Beautiful churches and schools everywhere
Wonderful cities both small and great
Making famous our Buckeye State
       My Ohio

Thoughts O' Mine

If I could only teach you
My wayward little son
To thread the thorny briers
That through your pathway run;

If I could only show you
The finer things of life
Could help you win the best here
Debarring sin and strife.

If I could only tell you
In the Savior's love abide
When sinful thoughts and evil
Surround at every stride.

Alas! I cannot follow
Your footsteps all the way
But I can teach and trust that
You will not go astray.

And I will strive to build you
So honest, kind, and true
You'll disregard the evil
That tempts and dazzles you.

And all those vulgar stories
That some men like to tell
I'd bury in the furnace
And ring their final knell,

For little ears will listen
And little tongues impart
Are grown-up folks aware of
The evil that they start?

Our little boys, such tiny tots
Our future men will be,
Then by precept build them now
The pride of liberty.

It's Spring in West Virginia

Written by Alice while attending Parkersburg High School on April 19, 1923

It's spring in West Virginia
The fairies all are near
For yesterday while out at play
I saw them working here
The little buds upon the trees
At last are wide awake,
A nest above the kitchen door
The robin tried to make.

It's spring in West Virginia
The fairies are around,
For with each seed a fairy came
From out the soft, warm ground.
A thousand little blades of grass
Are shining with the dew,
A thousand little fairies came
To greet the world and you.

It's spring in West Virginia
You feel it in the air
The sky has changed from gray to blue
The birds are everywhere,
A million little drops of rain
Are falling here and there
A million little violets now
Are blooming everywhere.

Playtime

When I was but a tiny tot
And sat on Mother's knee
She sang "Oh bye, baby, bye"
And nursery rhymes to me.

But now that I can walk and talk
And sit upon the chairs
We play that I am Goldie Locks
A-visitin the bears.

I am quite good at pretending too
And keep my eyes closed tight
But when the bears come prancing in
They open with delight.

And we both have older grown
Wherever we may be,
We'll play the games and sing the songs
We sang when I was three.

The sweetest songs and cherished games
Of childhood's first decade
Shall linger on in memory
And never never fade.

The Jericho Bridge

That old covered bridge is gone,
    And our hearts are sad today,
All we have—a memory,
    That old bridge is gone away.

'Twas there the wise old owl,
    In his midnight rendezvous,
Called far o'er the country side,
    Who-oo, who-o, who are you.

'Twas there where the hunters met,
    For to talk and laugh and sing,
And to hear the weekly chase,
    From the distant hillocks ring.

'Twas a place of foolish pranks,
    For the mischief-loving fads,
To emerge a witch or ghost,
    For to frighten timid lads.

Seventy years 'neath the storm,
    That old covered bridge has stood
Many heavy bulky loads,
    Have crossed o'er its floor of wood.

Let us cherish in our heart
    That old bridge of Jericho
And its merits ne'er forget
    As on through this life we go.

Spring Visions

The fields are being furrowed
The skies are bright and blue,
The morning sunshine glistens
Upon the frost and dew.

The hyacinths are creeping
Up through the rain-washed ground.
The daffodils are dancing
In every yard around.

A little maiden's singing
And walking in the sun,
And welcoming the spring time
And new life just begun.

Bluebirds are swiftly flying
From Southlands far away,
And of a house I'm dreaming
A house that's old and gray.

There, greenest vines are climbing
To hide a wee bird's nest
And there beside the garden
The flowers bloom their best.

'Tis there fond memory lingers
And fancied dreams are true
The high hills bright with sunshine
And high above the blue.

God's Garden

Note from Catherine Whelchel: I believe this poem was unfinished due to one additional line that would not have ended the poem. I did not include that line here.

God planted a rose in my garden
To tell of His wonderful love
Love that His Son had given
Ere He ascended above.

A lily grew by the wayside
Unfolding His face to the sun
To gladden the path of the stranger
Symbolic of God's Holy One.

God planted a fern by the brookside
Uplifting its fronds to the sky
Its dark green coolness of color
Is comforting passersby.

Untold Joy

In canning luscious golden pears,
And cleaning all the rooms upstairs
In planning work from hour to hour,
In growing some new plant or flower,
   I find a joy supreme.

While sewing garments new
And patching shirts and dresses too,
While washing dishes, making beds,
And combing little tangled heads,
   I find a joy supreme.

In doing some kind deed today,
And helping friends along the way,
While guiding youngsters at their play
And doing His will day by day,
   I find a joy supreme.

CPSIA information can be obtained at www.ICGtesting.com
Printed in the USA
LVOW092031181011

251096LV00002B/2/P